Painting with my father

poems by

Fran Baird

Finishing Line Press
Georgetown, Kentucky

Painting with my father

This book is dedicated to my wife, Bernadette

Copyright © 2019 by Fran Baird
ISBN 978-1-63534-826-2 First Edition
All rights reserved under International and Pan-American Copyright Conventions. No part of this book may be reproduced in any manner whatsoever without written permission from the publisher, except in the case of brief quotations embodied in critical articles and reviews.

ACKNOWLEDGMENTS

I want to thank Leonard Gontarek, mentor, friend, wonderful poet, extraordinary teacher

Publisher: Leah Maines
Editor: Christen Kincaid
Cover Art: Samir Tandon, Maia Baird
Author Photo: Samir Tandon
Cover Design: Annalise Baird

Printed in the USA on acid-free paper.
Order online: www.finishinglinepress.com
also available on amazon.com

Author inquiries and mail orders:
Finishing Line Press
P. O. Box 1626
Georgetown, Kentucky 40324
U. S. A.

Table of Contents

Painting with my father 1

Mud 3

What Does It Know 4

Dream & 5

Kwashiorkor 6

Stone Beach, Westport, Massachusetts 8

just because I waited long enough 9

Peel the Onion 10

The Writer's Son 11

Ménage 12

Renaissance Man 13

Ethnic Humor 14

Go Away, Interesting Obsession 15

Prometheus 16

Take My Advice 17

The Outer Banks 18

Stripping the paint from an old park bench 19

When You're Gone 20

And she asked 21

Not sent 22

Mysterioso 23

September Mourning 24

Narcissus 25

Desperate Day 26

As If 27

Silent Night 28

To answer the question: Are you a spirit or a ghost? 29

Painting with my father

1.

We never talked sex, we were both shy.
I blamed him, too tired to teach
his seventh son. Once, he pulled a book
from his bedroom shelf, opened it cautiously,
began to read of birds and bees. He lay
on his bed, propped up with pillows,
I was on my mother's bed, separated
by a nightstand. My nervousness drove me
from my body and I looked down
on this scene, more afraid than he was.
He closed the book before he finished a page.
If you have questions just ask, but I never did,
content to listen to the lies of older boys.

2.

And then we entered the world my father knew,
the world of paint, where he taught me everything
he had to teach himself. Prepare the surface, protect
from spills, carry a rag in your pocket, use different
brushes for different tasks, control the paint starting
almost clean. Most important, in those oil-base years,
clean up, using thinner and linseed oil, saving brushes
and paint for the next job. (I just thought he was cheap.)
He gave me all the jobs that required patience, running
low himself. It was a perfect fit for me. I was young,
slow and dreamy, and he called me *Rembrandt*, more
endearment than annoyance.

3.

I remember the fuzzy focus of the morning light,
the way it entered bedrooms like a mist,
the slanting rays of the long afternoons that cast
the crosses of the window frames onto splattered drop cloths.
I caressed the half-moon molding where the floor,
ceiling, and the walls would meet, with the creamy edges
of paint, spreading thick enamel carefully onto sanded wood,
the tip of my brush trembling. As the sun set, we cleaned up
and my father would extract this promise from me.
Stay in school, you don't want to do this all your life.

4.

Oh father, I want to do this all my life. Stare, as the sunlight pours through every window. Watch, as the slant of shadows paints the world. Love, with the gentle touch you taught me.

Mud

Winter is giving up but not without a fight.
Snowmelt runs in rivers in the street, grass
is breathing brown, and the dog looks guilty
as I wipe her feet, by the door you slammed
when you left. I'm already dreading the heat,
the temperature not yet fifty. That gray sky
that will skip to shimmering white in summer
reminds me that blue was never my color,
more like a state of mind. As for you, I'll
just scream and throw mud at your back
as you walk away. There'll be fistfuls plenty
by the time we get around to saying *sorry*.

What Does It Know

It takes us up the roughest path in the mountain

to a height where we gasp for air,

forcing us to breathe and rest.

It shows us the cliff, the air,

whispers to us,

convinces us we can fly.

We jump and spread our arms,

hit the water far below,

pushing our eyelids open, no choice

but to look at how deep we are going.

When faith runs out,

and we are drowning,

we break the surface.

Are we swimming to shore?

Are we climbing up again?

Dream &

I cross over the river of stars & there
my sister waits. In her hand she holds
the rainbow of the night. *I traveled
back, she says, to mother's womb &
there was filled with sight beyond my
birth. I became a speck. I come to
tell you this, for I knew that you
would understand. You, who I never
understood, you, who replaced me &
were loved. You, who I never loved.*

Kwashiorkor

In the language of coastal Ghana, *kwashiorkor* means *the sickness a child acquires after the next baby is born.*

I was the baby. My sister, the one before me, never looked me in the eyes, always above my head, right or left, past my ears. I was never sure she loved me.

Before I was born, she was father's favorite for eight long years. In a photograph, face tilted back, her eyes stare at the camera in front of our row home, smiling at the sky, a smile that disappeared when I was born.

Dad had a pet name for her. *Two pounds of sugar with the string tied tight.* His name for me was *Angel Divine*.

When he died, she could only call him *bastard*, brothers shushing her over lunch, me telling them *leave her alone she needs to vent*, while she laid out her complaints, his temper, his gambling that robbed her of comfort and gifts that she blamed for her pursuit of wealth she never found.

Years later she fainted. They found a tumor on her brain. Nine months after that she was gone. Before she died I saw her twice. The first time was at a party at another sister's house. We were in the same room for a half hour before I knew it was her, a stylish turban wrapped around her head hiding surgery scars. The last time it was at her home after she lost peripheral vision. I had to kneel before her chair so I could look at her and she could tell me, clearly, looking above my head once again, her husband and children within earshot, *I'm surrounded by assholes.*

And in between these times, there was a phone call, as if then she could speak directly to me, no need of eyes, to the brother she never understood (*France,* she use to say, *I don't get you.*) This time she told me where the tumor had taken her. *I went back,* she said, *I kept going back. I was a little girl. Then, I was in mother's womb, could feel myself there! And then, I was a dot.*

I put this in another poem where she visits me in a dream. But this is no dream, this is memory. In that other poem I have her say she never loved me, but I know that isn't true. We were the youngest in a horde of children trying not to die of hunger.

Stone Beach, Westport, Massachusetts

A tumbling girl holds two fists of stones
close to her mother's grin. The mother
shakes her head and the girl opens her
fists. The stones have lost their appeal.
They leave the beach, no look behind.

I gather the discarded, place the stones
in my mouth to wet them, to discover
what is hidden in their veins beneath
dried salt – jasper, onyx, opal and jade.
At home, I throw them in the tumbler
beside the whetstone, begin polishing.

just because I waited long enough

the sun left the sky long ago
island clouds, once mango,
are now sliced darkness

my children lose interest
the yellow day is gone,
time to turn home

their backs are to the shadow folds
in the cloud that remains
rising like a grey snowy mountain

light pink begins to appear
brushing the creases,
just because I waited long enough

Peel the Onion

Today's storm brushed clouds away,
a breeze removed the brittle heat.

The sky emerged Pacific blue,
air sweet with salty fragrance.

I hold the milky onion in my hands,
see the sun outline each layer.

As tears fall, I peel the onion.

The Writer's Son

Do you want to know my earliest memory? You were going off on one of your rants and I was scared. Not exactly scared, I just wanted to escape the noise, your shrill voice, so I crawled under the dining room table, the one you shellacked with all of your rejection notices. I looked up and the bottom of the table was shellacked with them as well. And I think this was the first time that I recognized I could read, I could really tell what the words meant without pictures. I was four or five, I'm not really sure what age, and I read, "You are not what we are looking for, we can't really use what you have to offer." I don't know when it started, but at some point, and I think it was after this moment, those words, I took them into myself and they became what you, what the world was saying to me. "You are not what we are looking for." Soon those words, that voice who was speaking, became mine.

Ménage
> *Woody Allen explains to Ingmar Bergman why he married his almost daughter.*

Love and Death were looking hard
for Lust to make a trio. Lay
in wait to make a date. Then far
from Death blind Love did stray, so far
he did not see Lust's long regard.
Lust's brush with Death made Love decay.
Love looked like Death, so it was hard
for Lust to make their triolet.

Renaissance Man

Clever, cleaver boy,
I stroll along with the times,
leave the addict behind,

chart the distance between
Ching bubble and Kabbalah boom.
Got a painter's sensibility with Tourette's of the heart,

don't know what's real or precious anymore.
I search for a confessor, while
a brittle prayer forms me.

Ethnic Humor

My father spoke Polish before he spoke English. His mother was German. I never understood where the Polish came from. Every time he made a mistake, hitting his thumb with a hammer, he'd say, *No use being Polish if you're not stupid.* He told me you're allowed to tell an ethnic joke if you're from that ethnic group.

My first wife's grandmother had a wicked sense of humor, heavy on the wicked, like a strudel soaked in butter that bypasses the stomach and goes straight to the heart. She was some kind of German extraction, extracted before the war, the Big One that her generation gets slobbered over for winning, as if they had choices.

I showed up at the bridal shower, having dodged the bullet of Vietnam, to transport the booty. My fiancée showed me Grandmother's gift, a fancy box with the Eiffel Tower on the outside and, inside, a miniature guillotine with the inscription, *French Birth Control.* We laughed but I was a little embarrassed. My Irish mother was not amused.

Years later, Grandmother's daughter, my then ex-mother-in-law, shows up at my aunt's funeral, for what reason I still don't know, after I left her daughter for another woman. She was all deadly smiles, baring her teeth like a dog, and when I went to kiss her hello she almost bit me. Germans, they have no sense of humor.

Go away, interesting obsession

You, you inconvenience, when will you come
at a decent time, allow me a good night's rest?
Why do you suppose you call it dreaming?

Prometheus

You promised us.
You promised fire.

I bring them fire every night, hide
the wound that hangs like a tongue,
thirsting for its own water.

Take My Advice

I stare out of windows,
forget to describe what I see.
Too often it is enough just to look.

My daughter sleeps till noon
then moves as if her dreams
were some kind of life she is living.

She blinks when I tell her,
*they will seduce you into
believing they are enough.*

Late that night, light spilling
from beneath her door, it is
not so easy to fall asleep.

The Outer Banks

You were above me, like the night, like the stars.
Unlike the stars, I could reach up and touch you,
hold the constellation of your breasts as you rose
up and down, while the Outer Banks stood guard,
kept the sea at bay. Stars I had forgotten watched
as we made love, far away from any telltale lights.

In the darkness, a light filtered through our tent.
There was no moon and the stars could not shed
such light. The light was you rising into the night,
and suddenly I was in love again.

In the light you bit yourself and I rose to meet
this revelation, a woman with no filter, such
sexual desire, she had forgotten all decorum.
You had taken love and flung it to the stars.

I started to reach my climax and you rose screaming,
throwing off the tent, forgetting nakedness as light
that came from the bar on the pier glistened on your
skin. I looked up, stars haloing your head, and we
laughed as sand fleas bit us uncovered on the beach.

Stripping the paint from an old park bench

We're getting old,
have *world enough and time*
to strip the peeling paint off the park bench in the yard.

Do you remember those days?
First married, when the life created
felt like this, scraping away layers of how it should be,

how everyone else did it,
what everyone else thought it should
look like. A marriage, a life. We had Saturdays to do

anything we thought
worthy of our time, spent an entire day
watching the sun lay its shadows across the yard,

and we thought how like the sun we were.

When You're Gone

When you're gone, of course I'll miss you,
but it will be more than that. The earth will
shift, tilt toward the sun. Before the darkness
descends, all will be revealed in a harsh light.
I will think you are still here. When the air
implodes, light will cease, and I will
live my life as if I have nowhere to go.

And she asked

And the singer asked, *What would it look like if we had peace?*
Someone said, *Like childhood, when I played in the streets…*
Added, *… without a care.* Someone said, *Old people, sitting on
Porches, watching young girls flirt and kiss the boys, the boys
Looking over at the porches, smiling, lifting their hats, asking
The old ones for their blessing.* And another said, *It would be
The taste of homemade peach ice cream sliding down my throat.*

I sat among them thinking of my day. How the smooth sky spread
High and wide and blue. How the columns of the clouds rose up,
Like white tornadoes, to challenge the blue above them. I looked up
At the painted sky all day, and felt its enormity seep into my mind,
Never thought of looking down, or over my shoulder, never thought
To press my back into a wall, nor check the exit sign on any door
Leading out of there. Peace was all around me, and I was not afraid.

These thoughts never left my lips. I sat in the audience like a stone,
Until the singer became a song she sang with their words, blended
Their voices into hers and lifted us on the roaring wind of her voice.
What we all hoped for, what we missed from our past, what we saw
When we closed our eyes and listened to her voice, like the clouds
That day, was the challenge of the dreamed-of-peace, while her song
Filled the space this violent world has left where our hearts should be.

I left the church with a smile and many promises, and left that song
Hanging in the air. Outside, the labyrinth of Chester was bathed in
Its confounding darkness from which few escape. I drove through
The danger of her streets, until I found the familiar highway home.
When I arrived, the singer's song was almost gone. And so, I asked
My daughter, *What would it look like if we lived in peace?* Without
Pause, she replied, *Of course, it would be rain falling in a bright sky.*

Not sent

I read your letter to the senator, thrilled
at what you said. Outside, the rain keeps
falling. How predictable it has become,
the buying and the lying, forgetfulness
that even we, the Woodstock nation, we
yes, we were going to change that world,
beginning with ourselves. It has taken me
more than forty years to change. I'm beat.

Mysterioso

I don't know what to say.

I want my words to break a heart,
force tears to spill.

I'm trying to let those clouds speak
to me, but it's forced.

Eighty-eight keys on my piano, black
and white, I counted them. Mathematics
reduces everything to anemic understanding,
no sloppy beauty. Still, it's mysterious,
all those songs, from such limitation.

I'm trying to save my life
by being present. It's a bitch when there are
no answers, when the air is eighty-two degrees
with no humidity.

September Mourning

A cloud of starlings darkens a lane of sky,
    perches among still-green trees, shaking leaves with chatter,
        telling stories of places where winter will remain unknown.

My neighbor's old dog barks continuously,
    wanting to escape the morning cold that assaults her bones.
        Let her in! I want no reminders that the warmth is leaving.

Three doves appear outside my window,
    their brown summer feathers already turning a dusty gray.
        Shadows cut across the afternoon. I listen to their sad calling.

Narcissus

It is too easy to think that everyone is here for me.
I've had friends and family die from too much drink,
too many thoughts of suicide, too much of everything
the world withholds. How to use their deaths to keep
myself alive? The only way to go beyond myself is
to ask for the advice I never use.

I look into the mirror to see deeper than anyone cares to go.
The conversation I find there in my eyes soothes the loneliness.

Desperate Day

It's raining. We need it, but I'm no farmer.
A last leaf clings to its branch, waving
like surrender, waiting for its fall. I could
do anything or nothing at all, the difference
sticks in my mind to torture me.

As if

She talks of God in a way that makes Him appear so small. As if there were no mystery, as if gender wasn't anything but a jacket we wear. As if God cared so much for her, exclusive of all supplicants, that she stood out like a favored child. As if.

Silent Night

December 23rd, walking the dog
on a balmy night. Soon it will be
Christmas. It rained earlier, clouds
pile up like dunes, turning the sky
into a desert backlit by the moon.

Some slide quickly across the sky
pushed by the wind. The dog lifts
her nose, surprised as anyone with
the warmth. From behind a cloud,
the moon appears, like a new star.

I'm whistling Silent Night, the line
Savior Lord at Thy Birth running
through my head. I don't believe
any of it anymore; the Virgin Birth,
Christ, the Son of God, the Messiah.

In my Torah class, the rabbi reveals
the 25th day of Kislev, a celebration
of a festival borrowed from Canaanite
forbears, overlaid with the building
of the Temple in Jerusalem. Later,

it becomes part of Hanukah, Jews
as confused as Christians about their
history. And I think, *so much we all
have in common.* Clouds suddenly
form a blanket obscuring the moon,

the wind picks up and I turn around
and I'm hit in the face with water.
A squall drenches me and the dog,
is gone as quickly as it came. We run
home. I don't know what to think. Did

God or the universe just spit in my face?

To answer the question: Are you a spirit or a ghost?

If you are reading this, there is an afterlife, because
I promised myself when I was living that, when I died,
I would ask the questions that used to annoy my teachers.

(They would have to answer them. After all, they died,
and realized beings shed their pettiness and petulance
when they are in the after, right? By heavenly, at least,

afterly decree, they would not be allowed those looks
anymore. You know the ones, if you got them, you'd
die!) I would send my answers back to you in the form

of poetry because, well, you knew me as a poet and if,
say, I sent them as certainties and you suddenly started
making predictions, like who would live and who would

die, or solving those unsolvable, as of yet, math problems,
for which there are cash prizes, well it would catch you
by surprise, freak you out even, you might die, or worse,

be mistaken for some profiteer looking to make a quick
buck off of the gullibility of the masses or their fears
regarding the afterlife, what happens when we die. I just

want to say, in case you didn't know, I ain't no ghost.

Fran Baird was born in Philadelphia, the youngest of 12 children and the 7th son of Jim and Mary. He attended St. Joseph's Prep High School and graduated from St. Joseph's University with a degree in Psychology. He served 2 years in the United States Army as a Psychology Social Work Technician, first at Walter Reed Hospital, then at an Army medical clinic in Thailand. Later, he became a Certified Family Therapist and completed a doctorate at Temple University. Along with fellow poet Amy Small-McKinney, Fran studied with David Ignatow at the 92nd Street Y in New York City in the early 80's. He received a Judson Jerome Poetry Scholarship at the Antioch Writers' Workshop in Yellow Springs, Ohio where he studied with poets Cathy Smith Bowers, the North Carolina Poet Laureate from 2010-2012, as well as John Drury and Jamey Dunham. His poem "Neshaminy" was published in the Schuylkill Valley Journal in 2009 and nominated for a Pushcart Prize. He is a member of the Mad Poets Society in Philadelphia and currently studies with Leonard Gontarek as a member of the Osage Street Poets. In a wide-ranging professional career, Dr. Baird has been a medical social worker, a drug and alcohol counselor, and a grant writer. He is a founding Advisory Board member of the Montgomery County Poet Laureate Program started by poet and impresario Joanne Leva. He currently is an adjunct professor in the Criminal Justice Department at West Chester University and conducts a poetry workshop with inmates at Graterford Prison sponsored by the Prison Literacy Project of Pennsylvania; ten poems from five poets from this workshop were published in the Fall 2017 Schuylkill Valley Journal (V45). Fran plays the flute and sax in a cover band, The Part-Timers. He lives in Fort Washington with his wife, Bernadette. They have three grown children, Annalise, Maia and Evan.

Painting With My Father is a magnificent book. These are lived poems—and Fran Baird would not let them go out in the world until they reached the level of the experience. They took time. Hence, their wisdom and extraordinary beauty in the best tradition of Poetry.

There is brilliance and grace and nobility in this poetry, qualities that we recognize inhabit the man who wrote it. They are the products of a world that always leans toward the good and the poems are equal to it. They are reports from the other side in a music of language that is intelligent, inquisitive, celebratory and sure.

Let me recommend, along with the title poem, What Does It Know; Stone Beach, Westport, Massachusetts (where our poet is part Demosthenes, part Charon); Just Because I Waited Long Enough (light pink begins to appear / brushing the creases); Desperate Day; Take My Advice; Stripping The Paint From An Old Park Bench; and the great final poem of the collection, To Answer The Question: Are You A Spirit Or Ghost?

You can almost hear the comforting, soft strokes of a paintbrush expert and affectionate, as you turn the pages. It is a deep pleasure to watch Fran Baird work wonders in his poems.

    —**Leonard Gontarek**,
    Author of *Take Your Hand Out Of My Pocket, Shiva*

www.ingramcontent.com/pod-product-compliance
Lightning Source LLC
LaVergne TN
LVHW041507070426
835507LV00012B/1397